W9-ALM-066

For a free color catalog describing Gareth Stevens' list of high-quality books and multimedia programs, call 1-800-542-2595 (USA) or 1-800-461-9120 (Canada). Gareth Stevens Publishing's Fax: (414) 225-0377. See our catalog, too, on the World Wide Web: gsinc.com

Library of Congress Cataloging-in-Publication Data

Glibbery, Caroline.
   Join the total fitness gang / by Caroline Glibbery.
      p. cm. — (Good health guides)
   Includes bibliographical references and index.
   Summary: Introduces topics related to maintaining good health, such as skin and hair care, cleanliness, sleep, dental hygiene, and the avoidance of extreme weight loss diets, drugs, tobacco, and alcohol.
   ISBN 0-8368-2181-5 (lib. bdg.)
   1. Physical fitness for children—Juvenile literature. 2. Physical fitness for youth—Juvenile literature. 3. First aid in illness and injury—Juvenile literature. 4. Reducing diets—Juvenile literature. [1. Health. 2. Physical fitness.] I. Title. II. Series: Good health guides (Milwaukee, WI)
   RJ133.G53   1998
   613'.0432—dc21   98-26400

This North American edition first published in 1998 by
Gareth Stevens Publishing
1555 North RiverCenter Drive, Suite 201
Milwaukee, Wisconsin 53212 USA

This U.S. edition © 1998 by Gareth Stevens, Inc.
First published as *Join the Fitness Gang* in England with an original © 1998 by Quartz Editions, 112 Station Road, Edgware HA8 7AQ, U.K.
Additional end matter © 1998 by Gareth Stevens, Inc.

Consultant: Dr. Martin Wright, general practitioner
Photography: Kostas Grivas
Additional photography and artwork: Sue Baker/Deidre Bleeze
U.K. series editor: Tamara Green
Design: Marilyn Franks

U.S. series editor: Dorothy L. Gibbs
Editorial assistants: Mary Dykstra and Diane Laska

Printed in Mexico

1 2 3 4 5 6 7 8 9 02 01 00 99 98

Good Health GUIDES

Join the Total Fitness Gang

Caroline Glibbery

Gareth Stevens Publishing
MILWAUKEE

Contents

Introduction

Could you take care of a nosebleed or relieve muscle cramps? Do you know how important it is to keep warm if you're ever stranded in cold weather? In case of an accident, a basic knowledge of first aid is very important. Caring for your body, however, is not just something you should do in an emergency. You need to do it every day — and in every possible way.

The kids on the cover of this book couldn't look fitter! They realize that keeping their bodies in top condition is something worth working at daily. Hair, for example, needs daily care to keep it shining and free of dandruff.

The boy in the picture at the right is revolted by the smell of his socks — not surprising, since he has worn them two days in a row! Socks need changing every day. You need to wash properly every day, too, not only to prevent the spread of illnesses and infections, but also to control unpleasant body odors.

As boys and girls get older, their bodies start to perspire more.

In other words, they sweat! Daily use of an antiperspirant can help control the odor that usually goes with it.

Teeth also need daily care. If they are neglected, teeth can become stained, or chipped, or full of cavities. Your whole body, in fact, needs to be treated with care and respect.

This book offers helpful tips about taking care of your body and provides some basic first aid for treating injuries. So, get wise to health, and become part of the total fitness gang!

Make your face a Zit-free Zone

Q. WHAT CAN TEENAGERS DO TO CLEAR UP ACNE?

Once you reach your teens, you'll be lucky if you never get a zit, or pimple — most kids do. Why not start your anti-zit campaign now! You can do a lot to keep them at a minimum.

Ryan used to laugh at David's zits. Now he wished he hadn't. His own face was covered with them. He even had a crop of pimples across his shoulders. Meanwhile, David's zits had completely vanished.

SIGNS OF PUBERTY

Pimples, or acne, are a common reaction to the changes happening in your body around your teens. Teenage acne occurs because your skin starts producing more oil, and keeping it scrupulously clean and grease-free becomes much harder. As a result, your pores become blocked. Germs simply love this environment!

A little sunshine

Sunshine can help prevent zits — but be careful. Too much strong sunlight can cause serious skin diseases, even if you don't feel it burning you at the time.

The next thing you know, you have a pimple or two. Acne seldom leaves scars, however, if you don't pick at or squeeze your pimples, and it usually stops when you reach adulthood.

IT'S COOL TO BE CLEAN!

Ryan's skin quickly started to clear up after he began using a mild antiseptic soap that was recommended for problem skin by his local pharmacist. Sometimes, though, he developed a particularly problematic pimple that needed a dab of antiseptic cream or gel. The pimples on his back were harder to get rid of. Part of the problem was he couldn't reach them very well. Also, he had never thought to use a bath brush or a loofah to scrub his back — and the pimples formed. Then, one day, Ryan discovered he had a boil.

ON THE BOIL

Boils are larger than ordinary pimples and can be swollen and painful. They are caused by germs that gather in a hair root. If you develop a boil, don't touch it; have your doctor take care of it. Meanwhile, another tip for avoiding zits — don't share towels or washcloths!

No

You need to perspire, or sweat, when you get hot; it's the body's natural way to cool down. Sweating excessively, however, calls for action.

Your body has as many as two million sweat glands hidden under your skin. They are active all the time, even when you're asleep, helping your body stay at a steady temperature and rid itself of impurities.

Fresh sweat usually has a sweet smell, but the strength of its scent changes when you get overheated or when germs start to breed. A damp, sweaty environment is an ideal place for germs to grow — if they're given a chance. That's part of the reason you should shower or bathe every day.

Washing is especially important after exercising or playing sports because you will perspire more as your body tries to cool down. Clothes easily absorb sweat and can quickly develop an odor. The problem is you're the last person who can smell it.

If you sweat too much

When you sweat a lot, in hot weather or as a result of exercise, you need to replace the water your body loses so you don't become dehydrated. Drinking lots of water usually does the trick.

Q. WHY IS DRINKING WATER SO IMPORTANT IN HOT WEATHER?

sweat!

The time has come for some serious lessons in personal hygiene.

FIGHTING INFECTION

Excess sweat can have a particular effect on different parts of the body. Damp, unwashed feet, for example, can develop sore cracks between the toes. This condition is known as athlete's foot. It is a highly contagious fungal infection.

An itchy rash under the arms, or in the folds at the top of the thighs, is another form of fungal infection. People who play sports often get it if they sweat a lot and don't wash and dry themselves thoroughly enough afterward. This infection also is highly contagious.

Never sharing towels and washcloths is one way to try to avoid getting infections like these. If, however, you do get one, your doctor or pharmacist can advise you about treatments.

WASH AND GO!

Your skin is not self-cleaning; you must wash it with care. First, splash water on your skin to dampen it. Then rub soap between your hands to make a good lather. Finally, rub the lather all over your body. You can also wash using soap on a body brush, a sponge, or a washcloth.

Remember to wash all over — not just the parts of your body that show! Washing under your arms and wherever you have folds of skin is especially important because sweat is most likely to gather in these places.

Both boys and girls might want to start using an antiperspirant or deodorant. They will perspire a lot more as their teenage years approach and their hormones become more active. In a short time, all these changes become second nature, then coping with sweat is no sweat at all!

Wet and worried

People often sweat more when they're nervous, such as before an exam or at a job interview.

Get out of my hair!

Your hair, just like your skin, needs to be kept clean and in good condition.

Louise was scratching her head a lot lately, but Emma didn't seem to notice as they sat close together sharing a book in geography class. The next day, Emma was scratching, too. That evening, when her mother washed Emma's hair, she noticed some tiny yellow lumps along the hairline behind Emma's ears. Emma had nits!

Nits are the eggs of lice. Although mother lice are almost too small to see — unless you look very closely — they lay at least sixty eggs at a time. Hair is an ideal environment for them. The nits hatch quickly, and, two weeks later, some of them start laying their own nits.

Unfortunately, it is very easy to catch nits if your hair comes into close contact with the hair of someone who already has them.

Q. WHY SHOULD YOU AVOID SHARING A COMB OR A BRUSH?

NO DISGRACE

You shouldn't feel embarrassed if you catch nits. Lots of boys and girls get them at least once in the course of their school years. A doctor or pharmacist can recommend a shampoo that will help get rid of nits. You also can try using a fine-tooth comb after washing your hair, wiping the comb clean after each stroke. Comb through your hair this way every day for a week. Be sure to wash the comb each day — and never share it!

HAIR CARE

Hair needs care. To keep it looking good, wash it at least every few days with a mild shampoo. Be sure to rinse out all the lather. Brush and comb your hair regularly during the day, too, even if it is short.

Heat can damage hair and make it break very easily, so don't set your hair dryer at a temperature that is too high. Tints and dyes can be harmful, too, especially if they contain bleach. So, if you ever think about changing the color of your hair when you are older, think twice! Is it really a worthwhile risk?

DOWN WITH DANDRUFF!

Nicole took good care of her hair, but she still had dandruff from time to time. Wearing light-colored clothes helped hide the little white flakes that

Over the sink

Do you hate having your hair washed because you get soap in your eyes — and it stings? See if you can lean backward, instead of forward, over the sink. Shampoo is less likely to drip on your face from that direction. You might start enjoying having your hair washed — and your hair will certainly benefit.

landed on her shoulders, but she still hated them. Washing her hair didn't seem to help much. Sometimes, in fact, it seemed to make the dandruff worse.

Dandruff forms when the scalp starts working too hard at making new skin. The dead skin cells come off in showers of white flakes. The scalp can also become infected. The best prevention and cure for dandruff is using a special antidandruff shampoo. Vitamins A and B from foods such as milk, lean meat, and vegetables can help, too. Take care of your hair. Healthy hair is beautiful. It's your crowning glory!

Dieting can be dangerous

When you want to lose a little weight, be sure to get some advice from your doctor. You could be doing your body a lot of harm.

One day, Anna passed by a full-length mirror and thought her stomach was sticking out a little too much. A few days later, she weighed herself. She had gained three pounds. Three pounds wasn't very much, but Anna was upset.

Anna didn't know that it's perfectly normal to gain some weight just before a growth spurt, and that the body quickly uses up the extra weight. So, she decided she must be overweight and put herself on a strict diet. She ate almost nothing, which made her jumpy and bad-tempered. She snapped at her family and friends — and felt terrible! No one found out what was wrong until she finally fainted at school one day.

THE GREAT PRETENSE
For many young people, a crash diet like Anna's can be the start of a serious eating disorder called anorexia nervosa. Ten times as many girls as boys suffer from it, but boys are still at risk when they get the silly idea that they need to drastically change their body shape.

Anorexia nervosa sufferers often pretend they have eaten when they haven't. When they look in a mirror, they see themselves as fat, even after they have lost so much weight that all

their bones stick out. Their body image is entirely distorted.

When someone with this eating disorder gets very weak, he or she usually has to be hospitalized. The same is true for those who develop bulimia. People with bulimia binge on all kinds of fattening foods, then make themselves vomit so what they have eaten will not add any weight.

A HELPING HAND

Most often, it is teenagers who develop anorexia nervosa or bulimia, but younger children and adults can develop it, too. If you know anyone who seems to be having eating problems or who is overly concerned about a weight problem that doesn't seem to exist, try to persuade that person to talk to a teacher, a doctor, or a parent. He or she might need help desperately.

If you ever feel the need to lose a few pounds, remember that starving yourself is not the answer! Eat well-balanced meals regularly. Just cut down on sweet and fatty snacks; eat fruits instead — and exercise more. You soon will look good, and you'll feel as good as you look. Remember, too, there's nothing wrong with being a little round and cuddly anyway!

Take your doctor's advice

Anyone who really has a serious weight problem needs to see a doctor. In fact, anyone who wants to lose more than only three or four pounds ought to do it with a doctor's advice. The body needs regular amounts of the right kinds of foods to stay healthy. A doctor can recommend the foods you should be eating so your health doesn't suffer as you lose weight. A doctor might also refer you to a dietician, who is a nutrition specialist. Remember, losing weight is something that should only be done gradually. Being very underweight can also be dangerous.

A good night's

Do you stay up late, even if you're tired, then wake up yawning in the morning? Wouldn't it be more sensible to go to bed earlier and wake up feeling refreshed?

Everyone needs sleep. If you don't get enough of it, your thoughts become confused, and you might have trouble concentrating. If Simon had known that, he might not have failed his math test. He tried to make up for missed homework assignments and not paying attention in class by cramming for the test the night before — he was cramming half the night. When he finished studying, he was so tired he couldn't get to sleep. His head was spinning with all the things he had tried to learn. By the time he finally fell asleep, it was getting light outside.

When the alarm went off, he rolled over and tried to go back to sleep. He felt awful! His father had to get him out of bed. At breakfast, Simon tried to remember what he had learned the night before, but he had forgotten everything — even what he had known before he started to cram.

SLEEPING PATTERNS
Sleep restores you. Your body creates new cells and your mind sorts out all the things you've thrown into it during the day. That is why a good, regular sleeping pattern, with only occasional late nights, is so important. If, however, you have problems sleeping, here are a few tips.

Q. HOW MUCH SLEEP DOES AN AVERAGE 7- TO 11-YEAR-OLD NEED?

sleep

Don't eat a big meal just before you go to bed, and avoid drinking anything at bedtime that has sugar or caffeine in it, such as cola, tea, coffee, or even fruit juice. The sugar and caffeine in these drinks will keep you wide-awake for hours. A cup of milk, especially warm milk, might help you settle down. Make sure you're warm enough, too.

NIGHT LIGHTS

Lots of people — even adults — are afraid of the dark. If you are one of these people and being in the dark keeps you from getting to sleep, ask for a night-light. Night-lights give just enough of a glow to make you feel safe — even when you know there isn't a bogeyman under the bed!

To sleep well, you have to be comfortable and feel safe and relaxed. If that means

having a soft doll or a stuffed animal in bed with you, go ahead and have one — even if someone teases that you're too old for it. If you're ever upset at bedtime, try to figure out the problem before you go to sleep.

Light exercise might help you sleep better, too. Try a few stretching exercises, then relax and breathe deeply. Imagine you are slowly melting into your mattress. You'll be in dreamland before you know it and wake up refreshed in the morning.

Sleep needs

There are no hard and fast rules as to how much sleep a person needs. Newborn babies, however, usually sleep the longest — 20 hours or more each day. Children 7 to 11 years old probably need about 10 or 11 hours; adults need about 8 hours.

What a great Smile!

If you want to be complimented on your teeth, always give them the very best care.

Hannah had a toothache. She was in a lot of pain. Fortunately, her regular six-month appointment was the next day. The pain, her dentist discovered, was because of a cavity in one of her molars. Hannah needed a filling. The molar was at the back of her mouth in the upper jaw, so the filling wouldn't even show. The dentist also removed some tartar deposits that had formed along the gumline on some of Hannah's back teeth.

The dentist didn't hurt Hannah at all, and he told her she had a great smile. He also took some time to explain to her why caring for her teeth and brushing them at least twice a day were so important.

Q. WHY IS BRUSHING YOUR TEETH IMPORTANT?

Hannah had lost her baby teeth and already had most of her adult teeth. These teeth, the dentist told her, would have to last a lifetime — maybe as long as 80 years. Hannah didn't want to have to wear false teeth like her grandmother did.

CHOOSING A TOOTHBRUSH

The dentist showed Hannah the right kind of toothbrush to use. A toothbrush with a small head could reach anywhere in her mouth. The bristles should be fairly soft so they won't scratch the tooth enamel or gums. Hannah never thought much about her gums until the dentist explained that plaque — a mixture of bacteria, food, and acid — not only attacks the enamel of our teeth but also attacks our gums. Vitamin C helps keep gums healthy, so the dentist told Hannah to eat lots of fresh fruits and vegetables.

Crunchy fruits and vegetables also help clean your teeth. Apples and celery are especially good and are much healthier for us, as snacks, than candy. Sweet snacks will eventually rot your teeth if you are not very strict about brushing them.

FROM THE INSIDE OUT

Some foods that are good for your teeth work from inside — milk, cheese, yogurt, bread, and eggs, for example, provide important minerals, such as phosphorus and calcium. Even if you're a vegetarian, you can get enough of these minerals if you eat sensibly.

All the surfaces of our teeth need to be brushed for a full two minutes both morning and night. Better still, brush after every meal. Brush your teeth using toothpaste — one with fluoride is best.

Toothpaste cleans not only your teeth but also your breath.

The dentist let Hannah have some fun, too. He gave her some disclosure tablets and told her to swish them around in her mouth with water. When she spit out the water, the areas on her teeth that were covered with plaque had turned bright pink! She had to brush her teeth very carefully to get rid of all the pink coloring.

Hannah was lucky. Her teeth had grown in very straight. Some kids have teeth that are crooked or too crowded. A specialist, called an orthodontist, can fix them with braces that usually must be worn for a year or more. Braces might seem like a nuisance at the time, but, in the end, they're worthwhile to get a great smile.

Get flossing!

Pieces of food often get stuck between our teeth. Left there, they can cause decay. To remove them, brushing is usually not enough. Use a toothpick after you eat, and get into the habit of using dental floss. Floss is like thin string. Break off a piece, hold each end, and slide it up and down between your teeth.

Eye

Most of us take sight for granted, but it is extremely precious. Imagine what life would be like if you couldn't see!

Tim saw a blind man tapping his cane on the curb and asked if he would like some help crossing the street. The man thanked Tim and took his arm. When they got to the other side, the man gave Tim some advice. He said, "Take care of your eyes, young man." Actually, Tim had recently been having trouble seeing the blackboard at school. He usually sat near the back of the room and had to squint to read what the teacher was writing on it. He started to wonder if he needed glasses, so he asked his mother to take him to get his eyes checked.

SEEING STRAIGHT

Sight can change very rapidly, so you should have an eye examination every year or so. If, like Tim, you have trouble seeing the blackboard, you might be nearsighted and need glasses to correct your vision. On the other hand, if you have trouble reading this page without holding the book an arm's length away from you, you could be farsighted. Glasses can correct this vision problem, too.

An eye exam is nothing to be afraid of. An optometrist will look into your eyes with a special light and find out how well you can see different sized letters on a wall chart. If you need glasses, there are lots of different frames to choose from — most of them are very fashionable. You might be able to wear contact lenses, which are small, circular plastic lenses worn on the surface of the eye. They are almost invisible to anyone looking at you.

Q. WHY SHOULDN'T YOU RUB YOUR EYES?

strain

TIRED EYES

Whether you need glasses or not, you have to take care of your eyes in other ways. For example, your eyes will get tired and irritated at times. When this happens, you might be tempted to rub them, but don't! Rubbing can spread infections to them.

Your eyes get tired when you have been using them the wrong way. Don't sit too close to the TV when you're watching it. You should be at least 6.5 feet (2 meters) from the screen. Don't watch TV too long at one time. Watching for more than two hours a day is really too much. There are so many other interesting things you could be doing instead. Too many hours in front of a computer monitor are not good for your eyes, either. Take regular breaks, or you might end up googly-eyed like the boy in these funny glasses is pretending to be!

SHEDDING LIGHT ON THE MATTER

Read and do your homework in an area with adequate lighting — not too dark, not too bright. It might help to have a lamp on your desk or by your chair.

If your eyes get very sore, become bruised or bloodshot, or start to water a lot, it's time to see a doctor who can recommend suitable treatment.

You must protect your eyes from other forms of damage, too, such as sparks, splinters of wood, or splashes of chemicals. Whenever you're doing work that involves hazards like these — carpentry, for example, or a chemistry experiment — *always* wear goggles to protect your eyes. Don't risk losing your sight for any reason.

Sunglasses

On a very bright day, wearing high-quality sunglasses will cut down on glare and can keep harmful sun rays from possibly damaging your eyes. There is no need, however, to wear sunglasses indoors.

A. RUBBING YOUR EYES CAN SPREAD INFECTIONS TO THEM.

Drug

These three kids don't want to be recognized, but they still want to warn you about the very real dangers of drugs.

My real name is Frederick, but everyone calls me Zed. Although I'm only fourteen, I have to see a social worker every week because I've been in trouble with the police. It happened a month ago. A guy offered me some pills outside my school, and a boy dared me to buy them. I was lucky; I didn't swallow any, but I gave three of them to a friend. He's in the hospital and still unconscious. The police asked me to identify the man who sold the pills to me, and they arrested him. My message to you is: **If anyone offers you drugs of any kind, just say "no." I wish I had done that!**

Heroin, cocaine, LSD, crack . . . are just some of the many kinds of drugs you might have heard about. Some are pills; some are injected; others are smoked. Glue can be sniffed; it's a drug, too. You probably know that all these substances can be very harmful, but do you know just how dangerous they really are? These three kids want you to know that doing drugs simply does not make any sense.

Q. WHY ARE DRUGS DANGEROUS?

alert

I'm Maria, and I'm twelve years old. It's hard for me to tell you this, but my Dad's not living at home right now. He's in a clinic where they try to cure people who are addicted to drugs. He even stole money so he could afford to buy his drugs.

He lost his job and might end up in jail. I feel sorry for him, because I know he feels guilty that he let the family down so badly. I'm also very angry inside that this should have happened to us all. We were such a happy family before Dad took cocaine. Once he started, he couldn't stop. My message to you is: **Anyone who wants to join the total fitness gang should stay away from drugs.**

Hi! I'm Vanessa, and I have to admit I'm ashamed of myself right now. Last week, at my friend's eleventh birthday party, someone smuggled in some alcohol. I didn't want to seem childish, so I drank half the bottle. Now I know it was the most childish thing I could have done. My parents had warned me a lot about drinking wine, beer, or liquor, but I didn't take them seriously enough. I was violently sick — more sick than you can possibly imagine. I also had a terrible headache the next day. Mom and Dad were furious, and I've been grounded for a year. My message to you is: **Alcohol can be bad for you and might be addictive, like drugs. That's why the government has such a strict age limit to buy it or drink it.**

A. DRUGS CAN HARM YOU PHYSICALLY AND MENTALLY; THEY ALSO ARE ADDICTIVE.

Feet

Your feet have to carry you thousands of miles in your lifetime, so giving them regular care is very important. Always try to wear comfortable shoes, starting at a young age.

Joy was excited when she was asked to participate in a sponsored walk. A local charity was trying to raise money to buy a special wheelchair for a disabled young boy. Helping such a worthy cause would be great, Joy thought, and the exercise would be good for her, too.

Joy's mother readily agreed, but she knew five miles was a long walk, and she wanted to be sure Joy didn't get blisters on her feet. She bought Joy a new pair of comfortable athletic shoes and also suggested she wear thick cotton socks to absorb the sweat from her feet.

A SENSIBLE APPROACH?

Joy, however, wanted to show off her sandals to some friends who were also taking part in the walk. Her sandals were very fashionable, with narrow leather straps and open toes and heels. When she saw them, she wanted them so much she didn't tell her mother that the straps rubbed a little under her ankles.

On the day of the event, everyone walked the full five miles, and they raised enough money for the wheelchair, but

Q. HOW SHOULD YOU CUT YOUR TOENAILS?

first

Joy came home in absolute agony. She wished she had listened to her mother!

She should have worn her new athletic shoes. Her sandals looked ridiculous with jeans and a sweatshirt, anyway. Now she had blisters on her ankles, and her feet ached terribly.

As she sat soaking them in a tub of warm water, Joy looked down at her feet and suddenly realized how marvelous they were. She decided to start putting her feet first and, in the future, to wear shoes that were comfortable, instead of just fashionable. If she did, her feet would soon be in good shape again.

FITTING SHOES

Fit feet need shoes that fit. When you buy a new pair, be sure there is enough room in the toes for some growth, but don't buy them so big that they slip up and down at the heels. Avoid very high heels, too. They push your toes into the front of your shoes, which puts too much pressure on them.

Never share shoes with anyone. Shoes that have been worn by someone else have taken on the shape of that person's feet. Also, fungal infections can be passed around when you share shoes.

Wash and dry your feet at least once every day. When you cut your toenails, always cut them straight across. Cutting them down at the sides might expose them to infection.

A. CUT YOUR TOENAILS STRAIGHT ACROSS, DON'T CUT THEM DOWN AT THE SIDES.

Please don't

Just look at the dirty ashtray in this picture! All the cigarettes you see were smoked by only one person in a single morning. Is it any wonder that most nonsmokers agree smoking is a disgusting, unhealthy, and antisocial habit?

It isn't grown-up to smoke. In fact, most adults who smoke would gladly give it up. The trouble is, they don't have enough willpower. They are addicted to the nicotine in cigarettes.

Pete thought he was pretty cool when he finally managed to inhale cigarette smoke. When he first started, smoking made him feel sick and dizzy — although he wouldn't admit it to his friends. Now, at only twelve years old, he was puffing away as if he had been doing it for years.

Pete started smoking when some boys on the playground dared him to take a puff. He didn't have the courage to refuse, because he wanted to be part of their group.

A DEADLY WEED

Tobacco contains an incredible number of different chemicals. Although none of them, by itself, will kill you outright, medical research has proven that smokers are much more likely to suffer a range of potentially deadly diseases, such as lung cancer and heart trouble.

If Pete keeps smoking, within a few years, he might start coughing a lot. He might also develop bad breath and an awful

Q. WHY SHOULDN'T YOU START SMOKING?

smoke!

taste in his mouth. By smoking, Pete is not only affecting his own health, but also the health of others. People who are around him when he smokes inhale the smoke he exhales. That's why smokers are not always welcome in many restaurants and other public places. Many of these places that do allow smoking restrict smokers to certain areas if they want to light up. If you have a friend like Pete, try to get the message across to him or her before it's too late and the person gets hooked on smoking. Although adults are free to choose whether or not they want to smoke, it should be clear to most of them, by now, that cigarettes are bad for everyone!

Kicking the habit

Did you know that if your parents smoke when you're close by you could also be breathing in harmful fumes? Try to get them to quit smoking. In the end, they just might thank you for being so caring. Here are some tips to help you talk to them:

• Explain your point of view as strongly as you can without being rude.

• Talk it through with them and tell them how much healthier they will be if they stop smoking. Promise them you will never be crazy enough to start smoking.

To the rescue

This book has a lot of helpful information on how to be and stay healthy. Any member of the total fitness gang, however, needs to know, also, what to do in case of an accident or medical emergency.

Joel tried to hit the baseball, but he missed, and the ball hit him right on the nose. Blood started dripping down the front of his shirt. Joel had a nosebleed. Fortunately, his friend Sam knew what to do.

Sam made Joel sit down with his head bent forward to keep him from swallowing any blood. Then Sam showed Joel how to pinch together the soft part of his nose. Joel was already breathing through his mouth, so Sam just reminded him to stay quiet and calm. Sam also told Joel not to swallow, cough, spit, or sniff if he could help it.

After about five minutes, Joel's hand was tired from pinching his nose, but, by then, the bleeding had stopped. Sam advised Joel not to blow his nose for a few hours. It might make the bleeding start again. If the bleeding hadn't stopped so quickly, Sam would have known to get medical help.

OUCH! IT'S A CRAMP!

After Joel's accident, both boys went indoors to watch TV. They watched a show

Coping with emergencies

What should you always remember if you find yourself at the scene of an accident? One of the most important things to remember is not to panic. Try to keep the accident victim as calm as possible. Also, be sure you know the telephone numbers to call for an ambulance, the police, or the fire department, and always give the address of your location very clearly. Your family should have a well-stocked first aid kit, both at home and in the car. Taking it on vacation with you is a good idea, too.

Q. HOW SHOULD YOU TREAT A MUSCLE CRAMP?

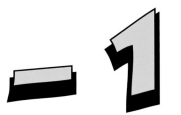

about two secret agents who were chasing some diamond thieves. In one scene, the thieves were running when, suddenly, one of them fell, clutching his leg. He had a cramp. Sam smiled. The same thing had happened to him a few days ago during a soccer game.

The thief's leg hurt a lot, so another thief stopped to help him, massaging the cramped muscle and straightening out the leg. Soon, both thieves were back on their feet running.

Cornered by the secret agents, one thief tried to hide the largest diamond by putting it in his mouth, but he choked on it, just as if he had swallowed a fish or chicken bone. His lips turned blue, and he was about to

collapse, when one of the secret agents realized what was going on. He bent the thief forward and thumped him hard on the back, four times between the shoulder blades. Whoosh! The diamond came out and the thief could breathe again.

Sam was so excited by the movie he got the hiccups. Joel made Sam hold his breath while he counted slowly to ten. When this didn't work, he suggested Sam try drinking water out of the far side of a glass. Miraculously, Sam's hiccups stopped just as suddenly as they had started.

Don't risk it!

Don't ever swallow anything you're not sure about! Some plants, such as certain berries and mushrooms, are poisonous. Get anyone who might have swallowed something poisonous to a hospital quickly.

A. RUB THE CRAMPED MUSCLE AND SLOWLY STRAIGHTEN OUT THE LIMB.

To the rescue

How much do you know about first aid? See if you know the correct procedures for the following situations.

The mayor's office was packed with newspaper reporters and photographers. Three young people stood proudly, waiting to receive their Junior Good Citizen awards. The first award went to Jason Cooper who, at only eleven years old, had saved the life of his best friend, Harry.

Months earlier, the boys were hiking with a school group when the weather suddenly turned stormy and cold. Harry and Jason somehow got separated from the rest of the group, and Harry stumbled into a pond. Jason managed to pull Harry out, but soon afterward, Harry started turning blue.

Fortunately, Jason knew from a first aid course how important it is to keep the person warm in these circumstances. The boys huddled together under a blanket

Jason had in his backpack until rescuers found them.

A BAD FALL

The second Junior Good Citizen award went to ten-year-old Polly Johnson. Polly was on her way home from school one day when she found her elderly neighbor, Mrs. Browning, lying on the sidewalk. Mrs. Browning had slipped and could not move. She was in terrible pain and thought her leg was broken. Polly ran to her house and called for an ambulance. Then she grabbed a blanket and ran

Accidents happen

Accidents happen when you least expect them. Check around your area for a junior first aid course you can take to learn as many emergency procedures as you can.

Q. WHAT SHOULD YOU DO IF A PAN CATCHES FIRE?

back to Mrs. Browning. Polly knew that a person in shock should be kept warm. She covered Mrs. Browning with the blanket and talked with her to keep her calm. A few minutes later, the ambulance arrived. Mrs. Browning was rushed to the hospital. Polly had not tried to move her, knowing it might only make matters worse.

UP IN FLAMES

The third Junior Good Citizen award went to nine-year-old Ben Watson. One Saturday afternoon, Ben's mother was cooking, and the pan suddenly caught fire. Ben's mother panicked and was about to take the pan to the sink to run cold water over the flames, but Ben stopped her. He had recently completed a course in emergency procedures and knew that pouring water on a cooking fire was the wrong thing to do.

Ben grabbed some baking soda and threw it on the flames. Then he soaked a towel with water and told his mother to hold the lid of the pan with it so she could cover the pan and smother the flames.

The fire went out, but the kitchen was full of smoke. Ben opened the windows to let in some air. If the fire had not gone out, Ben knew they had to get out of the house quickly and call the fire department from a neighbor's house.

Ben's mother's arm was burned slightly, so Ben made sure she put it under cold water to cool it down. A little later, he went to the hospital with her to have a doctor treat the burn. Thanks to her son, Mrs. Watson now knows exactly what to do if a pan catches fire. If Ben had not known what to do, the whole house could have gone up in flames.

Glossary

addictive — capable of causing an uncontrollable need for something, often a harmful substance, such as nicotine or alcohol.

antiseptic — able to prevent the growth of germs and bacteria that can cause infections and diseases on the skin or other body tissues.

boil — (n) a painful, infected skin gland that is red and swollen and forms a thick yellowish material, called pus, inside.

contagious — "catching;" able to be spread or passed on by contact, such as touching or sneezing.

cramp — a painful muscle spasm, or tightening, that can be caused by a sudden chill or by using the muscle too much.

dehydrate — to lose water or fluids from the body.

fungal — caused by or having a fungus, which is a plant that can survive only by living on other plants or animals, because it cannot produce its own food.

gland — an organ or group of body cells that takes substances out of the blood and changes them for use by the body or to be given off as waste.

hormones — substances, produced by glands and organs in the body, that are carried through the body by blood and other fluids to assist with human functions, such as growth.

hygiene — the rules and practices of keeping clean and staying healthy.

infection — injury to body tissues caused by bacteria, viruses, or other living things that produce diseases.

lice — tiny, flat, wingless insects that cling to the skin and hair of warm-blooded animals, including humans, and suck blood for food.

loofah — a sponge made from the fiber of loofah fruit, which is a tropical plant in the gourd family.

molar — a large tooth at the back of the mouth that has a rounded surface and is used for grinding food.

nicotine — a poisonous substance that comes from tobacco.

optometrist — a vision specialist who examines the eyes for problems and defects and prescribes lenses or exercises to correct them.

plaque — a slimy film that forms on the surface of the teeth and contains bacteria that can cause cavities.

puberty — a time of growth when boys and girls are changing physically and emotionally to become men and women.

revolted — repelled, or forced away, from something disgusting or shocking.

tartar — a yellowish, hard substance that forms on the teeth and comes from leftover food particles mixed with saliva.

More books to read

The Body Book. Sara Stein (Workman)

Care for Your Body. Staying Healthy (series). Rhoda Nottridge (Silver Burdett)

Come See What First Aid You Can Do. Foundations in Health (series). Jeanne M. Scott (The Visual Mentor)

Drinking Alcohol. What Do You Know About . . . (series). Pete Sanders and Steve Myers (Millbrook Press)

Good Health Guidelines (series). Catherine Reef (TFC Books)

Hair Flair. Dianne Balasco (Troll Communications)

Keeping Clean. Daisy Kerr (Watts)

Know about Drugs. Margaret O. Hyde (Walker and Company)

Sleep on It! Kevin Kelly (Children's Press)

Smoking Overview (series). David Pietrusza (Lucent Books)

Tooth Fitness: Your Guide to Healthy Teeth. Thomas McGuire (Saint Michaels Press)

Under Whose Influence? The Decision Is Yours (series). Judy Laik (Parenting Press)

A Unique Health Guide for Young People. Betty Y. Ho (Juvenescent Research)

Videos

Can You Tell Me . . . What Are Drugs? (Churchill Media)

The Clean Club. (Churchill Media)

Feeling Fine. (January Productions)

First Aid - Safety for Kids. (Churchill Media)

Peer Pressure. Teen Health (series). (Schoolhouse Videos)

Say No! (Human Relations Media)

Web sites

www.health.org/kidsarea/

www.optima-hyper.com/kidsafe.htm

www.kidshealth.org/kid/normal/

www.mrreach.com/

Due to the dynamic nature of the Internet, some web sites stay current longer than others. To find additional web sites, use a reliable search engine with one or more of the following keywords: *alcohol, drugs, first aid, germs, health, hygiene, sleep, smoking, teeth.*

Index